Music Minus One

4069

Arias
for
Tenor and Orchestra
from the repertoire of
Andrea Bocelli

A NOTE ON THE ARIAS

Verdi's *Rigoletto*, which was based on Victor Hugo's scandalous play *Le roi s'amuse*, premièred in Venice 11 March 1851, having twice been rejected by the Venetian censors. After the opera's première, and though it was an incredible public success in its homeland, it encountered still more problems as it traveled abroad. Its story of debauchery, vendetta and extreme tragedy was great fodder for Verdi but disgusted most censors of the time. Today, of course, the subject matter is hardly outrageous, though it is certainly disturbing, and it is of course one of the most popular operas in the Italian repertoire. And that success is due in no small part to one of its tenor arias, **"La donna è mobile."**

In the story, the hunchback Rigoletto has lured the debauched Duke of Mantua, who covets the hunchback's daughter, to a tavern and house of ill repute where Rigoletto has arranged to have him murdered. The aria, which Verdi set against a simple but very catchy tune, is scored in an exaggerated, almost circus-like atmosphere and Verdi has given the Duke a braggadocio perfectly suited to the character's dissolute nature and his attitude towards the female sex.

Another dark Verdi production, which appeared five years prior to *Rigoletto,* in 1847, was his adaptation of Shakespeare's *Macbeth*, the familiar tale of the ambitious Macbeth and his even more ambitious wife, who are spurred into a web of murder and deception by witches' prophecies of Macbeth's ascension to the throne. This masterful opera, which was Verdi's first attempt at adapting Shakespeare, brings us the recitative **"O figli, o figli miei!"** and magnificent aria **"Ah, la paterna mano."** It occurs early in Act Four, where Macduff has learned of the death of his wife and children, after which he plots his revenge against Macbeth, thus moving closer to fulfilling the witches' prophecies of Macbeth's eventual fall. Verdi's magnificent writing is enhanced by thrilling orchestration which proves the opera to be one of his greatest works.

Italy's other national hero in the world of romantic opera composition, Giacomo Puccini, would further enrich the repertoire for decades after Verdi's last works. Like Verdi, Puccini was fascinated by exploring new territories. And his greatest foray into exoticism, which consumed him the last five years of his life in the early 1920s, would become one of the most popular operas of the 20th century, *Turandot*. His work on it frustrated him so greatly that he would stop work on it for long periods, but he was finally able to bring it to near-completion just as he was diagnosed with throat cancer in 1924. He would never leave the Brussels clinic he entered for treatment, and the last two scenes of the opera had to be completed by Franco Alfano from Puccini's musical sketches. It remains the last major opera in the Italian romantic tradition.

In Calaf's third-act aria, **"Nessun dorma,"** the smitten prince ruminates over his imminent winning of the Princess in the game of riddles which he must survive. Puccini's rich coloring of melody and orchestration create a unique synthesis of western and eastern music, and at the same time of "old" and "new" musical styles, which help to make it, deservedly, one of the most popular tenor arias of all time.

Donizetti, in composing *L'Elisir d'Amore*, set out to create a successful *opéra comique* that would have lasting value, and he succeeded admirably in his goal. In fact it was the first of his operas to hold a steady place in the repertoire, a status it has retained since its première in Milan on 12 May 1832. In the memorable and justifiably famous aria **"Una furtiva lagrima,"** Nemorino sings an impassioned song of his undying love for the heretofore uninterested Adina. The aria is sung against the backdrop of an arpeggiated harp and a beautiful woodwind accompaniment, in which Donizetti masterfully uses a minor key to echo the depths of Nemorino's longing. Donizetti's masterstroke in this opera was knowing that the purely comedic songs must be counterbalanced by arias of real emotional import, providing the pathos necessary for a memorable and complete comedy.

From a lesser-known pen, that of Francesco Cilea, comes the relatively obscure opera, *L'Arlesiana*. When it premièred in 1897, it was a big success, and indeed, Enrico Caruso got one of his biggest hits from it, the beautiful *Lamento di Federico*, **"È la solita storia."** This aria is one of the high points of Cilea's output and is deservedly loved by tenors as well as audiences. It is one of those instances in which one aria eclipses its source, and it is sad that today Cilea's name is hardly known, his only opera to remain firmly in the repertoire being the more familiar *Adriana Lecouvreur*.

Franz Schubert's eternally popular **"Ave Maria,"** though originally presented in German and Latin, is given here in its much-loved Italian and Latin version. The song was part of a three-song cycle called *Ellens Gesang III,* and was written around 1825. Its simple beauty, which contains Schubert's trademark lyricism, is enhanced by the double-triplet accompaniment from the strings which lends an almost hypnotic effect to the song.

Any Italian tenor these days counts in his repertoire the Neapolitan song, *'O Sole Mio!* Written by Eduardo di Capua (1864-1917) and published in 1908, its heart-rending melody has an inescapable charm and grandeur to even the most jaded listeners, and it typifies the great warmth of the Italian spirit. In the hands of a good tenor, it is a magnificent experience, a perfect synthesis of operatic and popular idioms, and a perfect showcase for the tenor voice.

—*Michael Norell*

RIGOLETTO
"La donna è mobile"

Giuseppe Verdi

La donna è mo-bi-le qual piuma al ven-to, mu-ta d'ac - cen-to

e di pen - sie-ro. Sempre un a-ma-bi-le leg-gia-dro vi-so,

6

E sempre mi-se-ro chi a lei s'af-fi da, chi le con-fi-da

mal cau-to il co - re! Pur mai non sen-te-si fe-li-ce ap - pie - no

chi su quel se - no non li-ba a - mo - re! La donna è mo - bil

qual piuma al ven - to, mu - ta d'ac - cen - to e di pen - sier,

e di pen - sier, e,

e di pen - sier!

MACBETH
"O figli, o figli miei!...Ah, la paterna mano"

Giuseppe Verdi

11

l'ul_ti_mo sin_gul_to, col_l'ul_timo,coll'ultimo re_

spir. Ah! Tram_mi al ti_ranno in fac_cia, Si_ my

gno_re,e s'ei mi sfug_ge pos_sa a colui le_

brac__cia del tu_o perdo_no a_prir, possa a colui le

12

braccia, possa a colui le brac _ _ cia del tu _ o perdo_no a_

prir, Si _ gnor! pos _ sa a colui le braccia del tuo perdono a_

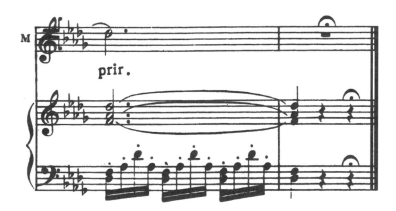

prir.

TURANDOT

"Nessun dorma"

Giacomo Puccini

14

15

MMO 4069

L'Elisir d'Amore
"Una furtiva lagrima"

Gaetano Donizetti

Un so - lo i - stan - te i pal - pi - ti

del suo bel cor___ sen - tir! I miei so - spir con -

fon - de - re per po - co a' suoi___ so - spir! I

pal - pi - ti, i pal - pi-ti sen - tir, con - fon - de - re i miei co' suoi so -

*This alternate cadenza has become traditional.

L'Arlesiana

"È la solita storia"
(Lamento di Federico)

Francesco Cilea

24

_g'io tan_to pe _ nar?.............................

Lei, sem_pre lei mi par _ la al cor... Fa _ ta_le Vi _ sion, mi la _ _ scial............................ Mi fai tan_to ma _ _ le! Ah _ i _ mè!

Ave Maria

'O SOLE MIO!

Eduardo di Capua

1. Che bel - la co - sa 'na iur - na - ta 'e so - le,___ n'a - ria se - re - na dop - - po 'na tem - pe - stal___ Pe' ll'a - ria fre - sca pa - re già 'na fe - sta....

2. Quan - no fa not - te e 'o so - le se ne scen - ne,___ mme ve - ne qua___ - se 'na mal - in - cu - ni___ - a,___ sotto 'a fen - e___ - sta to - ia re - star - ri - a,___